Kangaroos for Kids

by Judith Logan Lehne
illustrated by John F. McGee

NORTHWORD PRESS, INC.
Minocqua, Wisconsin

WILDLIFE *For Kids* **SERIES**

DEDICATION

To my now-grown son, Kyle, who was once a kyle-a-roo.

ACKNOWLEDGMENTS

I wish to thank Dr. David B. Croft of the University of New South Wales, Saul Markowitz and Henry Kacprzyk of the Pittsburgh Zoo, and Mela Kucera of the University of Maryland for the wealth of information they shared with me. Thanks also to my friend Pamela Kuck for her extensive, personal insights as a traveler into the land of kangaroos, and to my daughter, Tessa, for teaching me things about 'roos that I couldn't learn from research.

© Judith Logan Lehne, 1997

Photography © 1997: Hans Reinhard/Bruce Coleman, Inc., front cover; Jen and Des Bartlett/Bruce Coleman, Inc., 3, 15, 20-21, 47; Tom DiMauro/The Wildlife Collection, 6; Martin Harvey/The Wildlife Collection, 8, 10-11, 18, 30-31, 40, 44; John Giustina/The Wildlife Collection, 14; Martin Withers/Dembinsky Photo Associates, 16-17; Art Wolfe, 23, 34, 39; Chris Huss/The Wildlife Collection, 26; Gavriel Jecan/Art Wolfe, Inc., 28; Len Rue Jr./Bruce Coleman, Inc., 32; Joe McDonald/Bruce Coleman, Inc., 36-37; Norman Owen Tomalin/Bruce Coleman, Inc., 42-43; Tim Laman/The Wildlife Collection, back cover.

NorthWord Press, Inc., P.O. Box 1360, Minocqua, WI 54548

The **National Wildlife Federation**® is the nation's largest conservation education and advocacy organization. Since 1936, NWF has educated people from all walks of life to protect nature, wildlife and the world we all share.

Ranger Rick® is an exciting magazine published monthly by National Wildlife Federation®, about wildlife, nature and the environment for kids ages 7 to 12. For more information about how to subscribe to this magazine, write or call: Ranger Rick Department, National Wildlife Federation, 8925 Leesburg Pike, Vienna, Virginia 22184, 1-800-588-1650.

°National Wildlife Federation, 1997 ™ and ® designate trademarks of National Wildlife Federation are used, under license, by NorthWord Press, Inc.

Illustrations by John F. McGee / Book design by Russell S. Kuepper

For a free catalog describing our audio products, nature books and calendars, call **1-800-356-4465**, or write Consumer Inquiries, NorthWord Press, Inc., P.O. Box 1360, Minocqua, Wisconsin 54548

Library of Congress Cataloging-in-Publication Data

Lehne, Judith Logan.
    Kangaroos for kids / by Judith Logan Lehne ; illustrations by John F. McGee
        p. cm. — (Wildlife for kids series)
    ISBN 1-55971-595-2 (sc)
    1. Kangaroos—Juvenile literature. [1. Kangaroos.] I. McGee, John F. , ill. II. Title. III. Series.
QL737.M35L44 1997
599.2'22—dc21
                                    96-37145

Printed in Malaysia

Kangaroos for Kids

Gray kangaroo

by Judith Logan Lehne
illustrated by John F. McGee

If I told you I had seen a baby kangaroo the size of a bumble bee, you would probably think I was joking. The truth is, if I hadn't seen it with my very own eyes, I wouldn't believe it, either.

I'm Kyle, and I'm in the fourth grade. My sister Kate is a zoology teacher. Last year, she studied kangaroos in the Outback, a remote grassy region in Australia with more kangaroos than people.

I have lived in Australia all of my life, so I've seen plenty of kangaroos. Some people call them 'roos.

Sometimes they come right into our yard when we're sleeping, but I never knew much about them until I went to the Outback with Kate. That's when I saw the tiny 'roo.

Like humans, kangaroos are mammals. They are also marsupials (MAR-SOO-PEE-ALS), which means they raise and carry their babies in a pouch on their abdomens.

Imagine how handy it would be to have a giant pocket attached to your belly. No more lost baseballs or mittens!

Red kangaroo

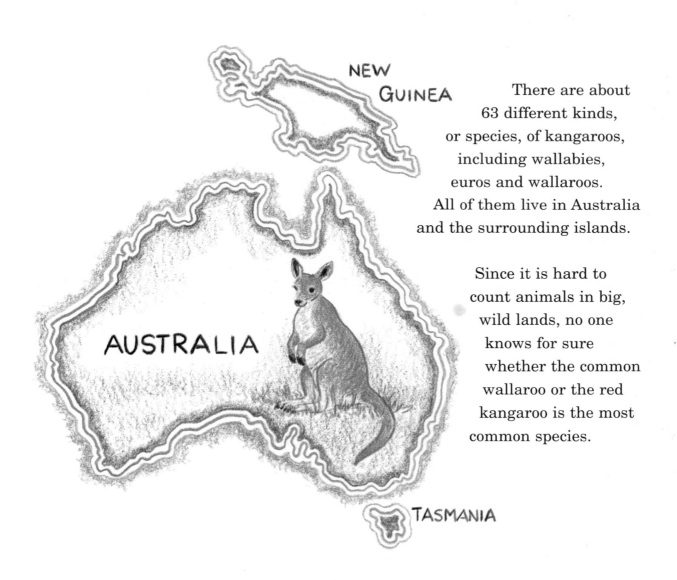

There are about 63 different kinds, or species, of kangaroos, including wallabies, euros and wallaroos. All of them live in Australia and the surrounding islands.

Since it is hard to count animals in big, wild lands, no one knows for sure whether the common wallaroo or the red kangaroo is the most common species.

Kate said there may be species no one has seen yet. For instance, the long-footed potoroo and the proserpine rock-wallaby weren't discovered until the 1980s.

We started our trip to the Outback. I couldn't wait to see some different types of kangaroos. I hoped I would discover a new species. If the scientists named it after me, they could call it a Kyle-a-roo!

Swamp wallaby

Kangaroos got their name accidentally. When Captain James Cook was exploring Australia in 1770, he was surprised to see strange hopping animals. "What are those creatures?" he asked the friendly native Aborigines (AB-O-RIJ-I-NEES).

They didn't understand Cook's question. "Kangaroo!" they replied, which is an Aborigine word meaning, "I don't know what you're saying."

From then on, the hopping marsupials have been called kangaroos.

When we finally arrived at our camp in the Outback, the first thing I saw was about twenty red kangaroos leaping through the dry grass. A group of kangaroos is called a mob.

Reds and grays are the largest kangaroos. Some males are over 7 feet tall and weigh more than 200 pounds. That's about the size of a professional basketball player! Red kangaroos can run over 40 miles per hour and jump up to 6 feet high.

I sure would like to have a kangaroo on my team!

Wallaroos and euros are rock climbing kangaroos. They are smaller than the grays and reds. Wallabies are smaller still, but the smallest adult kangaroos are rat kangaroos, which are about the size of large rabbits. The rare nabarlek, a tiny rock-climber, weighs only 2-1/2 pounds.

Kangaroos have soft, woolly fur of many different colors. Some have stripes on their head, back or arms. Red kangaroo fur is (surprise!) reddish-rust colored. Grays have long, silvery hair or short, dark gray fur. Wallaroo fur varies from dark gray to pinkish-brown.

Common wallaroo

Kangaroos aren't naturally very sociable or affectionate with one another, but most travel in small groups for safety. Whiptail wallabies are the most sociable, traveling in mobs of 50 to 100. Quokkas, also called short-tailed wallabies, like to be alone most of the time, only getting together at feeding areas or water holes.

Red kangaroo

As the mob of red kangaroos hopped across the plain, I studied their feet and legs. The two large hind legs are specially built for hopping. Looking at the big, back feet, it is easy to understand how kangaroos hop so well. The extra-long fourth toe (the middle one) pushes off for the great leaps.

The second and third toes are connected, and although they don't help much with hopping, kangaroos use them to comb their fur.

Tree kangaroos hop, too, but they have sharp front claws and short hind feet with special grip-tight skin that keeps them from slipping out of trees even when sleeping. They can make 30 foot leaps through trees to get their meals. Now that's fast-food!

Hopping takes lots of energy. If you don't believe me, try hopping instead of walking. You would be out of breath in no time. A kangaroo doesn't have to work as hard at breathing while it hops. Its stomach bounces up and down with each hop, automatically pushing air in and out of the lungs.

Large kangaroos can keep up a regular pace of 15 to 20 miles per hour, including leaps of 6 feet or more. They use their super-charged speed and longest leaps to outrun danger.

Rock wallabies have been called the prettiest kangaroos, and they have very powerful legs. A brush-tailed wallaby can leap more than 20 feet, then land, steady, on a narrow ledge.

Red kangaroo

When resting, kangaroos can use their long tails as chairs, but since the upper body is much heavier than the lower half, the tail also works as a counter-balance during hopping.

When kangaroos run, their tails bend at the end like a boomerang. As the tail moves up and down, it helps keep kangaroos from toppling over, head-first.

In late afternoon some kangaroos lie on their sides,
propped up on one elbow and forearm with their heads up.
They take short naps just like my father does on our sofa!

Some kangaroos crawl-walk. It's a funny sight! The kangaroo crouches over and puts its front feet on the ground. It uses its tail like an extra leg to balance, and the hind legs swing forward to take a step.

Besides hopping and walking, kangaroos also use their strong legs when they're in danger. They thump their feet on the ground to warn others in the mob.

And although they don't enjoy it, they can swim
if there's no other way to escape danger. They kick
with their back legs and use their front legs to
paddle to safety.

A kangaroo's front paws look a lot like fur-covered human hands. Their paws can grab long plant stems, and the curved claws hook food and bring it to their mouths.

During our stay at the Outback camp, Kate and I got up early to watch kangaroos feeding.

Kangaroos are nocturnal, which means they are most active at night. The musky rat kangaroo is the only species that is active during the day.

Gray kangaroo

Kangaroos spend a lot of time sleeping, but they rarely have any deep sleeps that last more than an hour at a time.

In the heat of the day, kangaroos rest in the forest and shaded areas of the prairie or in rock crevices. They pant and sweat and lick their arms to keep cool.

Most kangaroos are herbivores, meaning they are plant eaters. As Kate and I watched from under some eucalyptus (U-KA-LIP-TUS) trees, some of the kangaroos grazed, nibbling the green grass close to the ground. Others browsed along the edge of the field, tearing off pieces of eucalyptus leaves. Tree kangaroos even climb out on branches to get to their leafy meals.

Kangaroos may not have beautiful smiles, but pretty isn't important when you have to eat coarse grass and tough leaves.

Kangaroo teeth are specially designed to chew food thoroughly. The incisors (IN-SIZE-ORS) in the front cut the plants. The molars in the back chew and grind the food. Kangaroos shift food from one set of teeth to the other with their tongues.

The small bettong and the rat kangaroo are omnivorous, meaning they eat both plant and animal foods. Their incisors are more pointed, which helps them scoop up bugs.

If I were a kangaroo, I'd rather be a red or a gray because I wouldn't like eating insects for breakfast!

One morning Kate and I
watched a red kangaroo eat some
leaves from a eucalyptus tree.
As he tossed his head back, his
chest and abdomen suddenly shud-
dered. He was regurgitating his
food, which means re-chewing it to
break down the tough plant fibers.

It's a very lucky thing that
kangaroos have extra molars in
their jaws. When one molar falls
out, another tooth appears.
Kangaroos can grow as many as
sixteen new teeth for each one
that falls out.

Since kangaroos only live 6
to 10 years, they have enough
replacement teeth to last them a
lifetime.

Gray kangaroo

Kangaroos get some moisture from the plants they eat, but they are able to go for months without drinking any water at all. When it is time for a drink, the agile wallaby digs wells to uncover pools of water. He's a great neighbor to have if you're thirsty, since he's willing to share!

Even at night, kangaroos have terrific vision. Set far apart on either side of their narrow heads, their eyes can see most of the landscape at once while still noticing small movements far away.

Kangaroos have a keen sense of hearing too. The two ears rotate separately, taking in sounds coming from all directions. Their ears are constantly moving, even when they sleep.

Kangaroos need those sharp senses to help avoid their enemies. Besides humans, dingoes are the greatest danger to kangaroos.

These wild dogs sometimes kill dozens of young kangaroos in one attack. Wild cats, pythons, foxes, Tasmanian devils and eagles also prey on young kangaroos.

Kangaroos migrate, which means they move from place to place in search of food. They don't have permanent homes, but sleep wherever they can find summer shade and wind-protected winter shelters.

Rock wallabies are the only exception, sometimes making permanent homes in caves.

37

One night I heard clucking noises and a tongue-clicking sound. It was some kangaroos "talking."

Red kangaroos are usually silent, but grays can be quite noisy at times. For instance, during mating, the male clucks as he lays his paw on the female's shoulder and bobs his head. Females often cough or hiss at males, and mothers and babies "talk" to one another with clicks and clucks.

We also saw a female cleaning the inside of her pouch. She was getting ready for the birth of a new baby, called a joey.

Although Joey is a boy's name, all in-the-pouch babies are called joeys. When a baby kangaroo is out of the pouch full-time, it is called a yearling, or a joey-at-foot.

At any one time, a mother kangaroo can have a joey-at-foot, a newborn joey-in-the-pouch, and another baby waiting inside her body. She sure is a busy mom!

Red kangaroo

When the mother finished her pouch cleaning she tucked her tail under her. She rocked back on her haunches, and with our binoculars we could see her new baby underneath her. It was tiny, hairless and no bigger than a bumble-bee!

The newborn's eyes and ears were barely visible, but Kate said newborn joeys have well-developed nostrils and arms. Its little, sharp-clawed feet dug into the mother's belly-fur, and it began climbing up to the pouch.

It takes a tiny joey from 2 to 30 minutes to complete the 6 inch distance to the pouch. That may not seem like a long, dangerous trip to you, but you aren't the size of a bee!

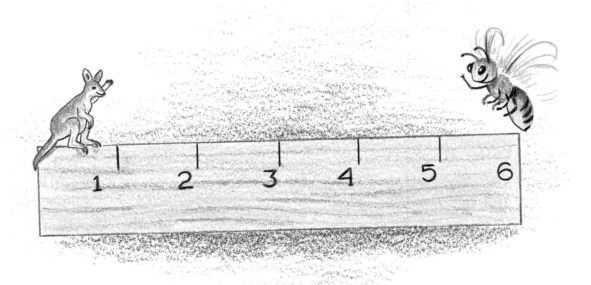

Kangaroo babies stay inside the mother's pouch for many days. Brush-tailed bettongs are fully developed in only 90 days, while it takes red kangaroo joeys 235 days to develop.

At age 6 months, the joey comes out of the pouch for a few minutes at a time. Each day the joey spends more time outside the hairless pouch. When it is time to climb back inside, the mother bends down and the joey pulls itself into the pouch.

The father kangaroo doesn't help the mother with her joeys. Young-at-foot joeys sleep close to their mothers and learn all of their kangaroo lessons from her.

Red kangaroos

Boxing and wrestling with older 'roos is playtime for young-at-foot joeys, but when an adult male must defend himself, it isn't a game.

Their arms look weak, but they have a powerful punch. Also, they can grab each other in a tight bear-hug.

If further challenged, they scratch with their sharp claws or lean back on their tails, using their rear feet to kick.

However, kangaroos are usually gentle creatures. They would rather run than fight.

The night before we had to leave the Outback, I sat alone under the moonless sky, listening to muffled thumping and the rustle of leaves in a tangle of trees.

I knew kangaroos were out there with me, even though I couldn't see them. I wondered if a tiny rat kangaroo might be hopping about in the darkness, using its tail to gather dried leaves and ferns for a nest.

I stayed outside until the moon came out, and I saw a gray kangaroo move across the field.

Then it was time for me to get hopping into bed!

Other titles available in our popular

WILDLIFE *For Kids* SERIES

See your nearest book seller
or order by phone 1-800-356-4465

NORTHWORD
NORTHWORD PRESS, INC.